Joseph Priestley

The present state of Europe compared with antient prophecies

A sermon preached at the Gravel Pit Meeting in Hackney

Joseph Priestley

The present state of Europe compared with antient prophecies
A sermon preached at the Gravel Pit Meeting in Hackney

ISBN/EAN: 9783337104870

Printed in Europe, USA, Canada, Australia, Japan

Cover: Foto ©Lupo / pixelio.de

More available books at **www.hansebooks.com**

The prefent State of Europe compared with Antient Prophecies;

A SERMON,

PREACHED AT

THE GRAVEL PIT MEETING IN HACKNEY,

FEBRUARY 28, 1794,

Being the Day appointed for a General Faſt.

By *JOSEPH PRIESTLEY, LL.D. F.R.S. &c.*

WITH A PREFACE,

CONTAINING THE

Reaſons for the Author's leaving England.

———

THIRD EDITION.

———

B. Quo fugis ? Expecta. Liceat condiſcere cauſas
Diffidii. Tu noſtra, puer, niſi fallor, amabas
Paſcua.
P. Parce, Parens, damnare tuum.—Tibi lætior annis
Tunc animus fuerat. Nunc intractabilis, aſper.
Petrarch on taking leave of his patron, the Cardinal Colonna.

Nos patriæ fines, nos dulcia linquimus arva.
Virgil.

———

LONDON:

PRINTED FOR J. JOHNSON, NO. 72, ST. PAUL'S CHURCH-YARD.

———

1794.

[Price ONE SHILLING.]

PREFACE.

THIS difcourfe, and thofe on the *Evidences of Divine Revelation*, which will be publifhed about the fame time, being the laft of my labours in this country, I hope my friends, and the public, will indulge me while I give the reafons of their *being* the laft, in confequence of my having at length, after much hefitation, and now with reluctance, come to a refolution to leave this kingdom.

After the riots in Birmingham, it was the expectation, and evidently the wifh, of many perfons, that I fhould immediately fly to France, or America. But I had no confcioufnefs of guilt to induce me to fly my country*. On the contrary, I came directly to London, and inftantly, by means of my friend Mr. Ruffell, fignified to the king's minifters, that I

---

* If, inftead of flying from lawlefs violence, I had been flying from public juftice, I could not have been purfued with more rancour, nor could my friends have been more anxious for my fafety. One man, who happened to fee me on horfeback on one of the nights in which I efcaped from Birmingham, expreffed his regret that he had not taken me, expecting probably fome confiderable reward, when, as he faid, it was fo eafy for him to have done it. My friends earneftly advifed me to difguife myfelf as I was going to London. But all that was done in that way was taking a place for me in the mail coach, which I entered at Worcefter, in another name than my own. However, the friend who had the courage to receive me in London had thought it neceffary to provide a drefs that fhould difguife me, and alfo a method of making my efcape, in cafe the houfe fhould have been attacked on my account; and for fome time my friends would not fuffer me to appear in the ftreets.

was

was there, and ready, if they thought proper, to be interrogated on the fubject of the riot. But no notice was taken of the meffage.

Ill treated as I thought I had been, not merely by the populace of Birmingham, for they were the mere tools of their fuperiors, but by the country in general, which evidently exulted in our fufferings, and afterwards by the reprefentatives of the nation, who refufed to inquire into the caufe of them, I own I was not without deliberating upon the fubject of emigration; and feveral flattering propofals were made me, efpecially from France, which was then at peace within itfelf, and with all the world; and I was at one time much inclined to go thither, on account of its nearnefs to England, the agreeablenefs of its climate, and my having many friends there.

But I likewife confidered that, if I went thither, I fhould have no employment of the kind to which I had been accuftomed; and the feafon of active life not being, according to the courfe of nature, quite over, I wifhed to make as much ufe of it as I could. I therefore determined to continue in England, expofed as I was not only to unbounded obloquy and infult, but to every kind of outrage; and after my invitation to fucceed my friend Dr. Price, I had no hefitation about it. Accordingly I took up my refidence where I now am, though fo prevalent was the idea of my infecurity, that I was not able to take the houfe in my own name; and when a friend of mine took it in *his*, it was with much difficulty that, after fome time, the landlord was prevailed upon to

transfer

transfer the leafe to me. He expreffed his apprehenfions, not only of the houfe that I occupied being
demolifhed, but alfo a capital houfe in which he
himfelf refides, at the diftance of no lefs than twenty
miles from London, whither he fuppofed the rioters
would go next, merely for fuffering me to live in a
houfe of *his*.

But even this does not give fuch an idea of the
danger that not only myfelf, but every perfon, and
every thing, that had the flighteft connexion with
me, were fuppofed to be in, as the following. The
managers of one of the principal charities among the
Diffenters applied to me to preach their annual fermon, and I had confented. But the treafurer, a man
of fortune, who knew nothing more of me than my
name, was fo much alarmed at it, that he declared
he could not fleep. I therefore, to his great relief,
declined preaching at all.

When it was known that I was fettled where I
now am, feveral of my friends, who lived near me,
were ferioufly advifed to remove their papers, and
other moft valuable effects, to fome place of greater
fafety in London. On the 14th of July, 1792, it
was taken for granted by many of the neighbours,
that my houfe was to come down, juft as at Birmingham the year before. When the Hackney affo-
ciation was formed, feveral fervants in the neighbourhood actually removed their goods; and when
there was fome political meeting at the houfe of Mr.
Breillat, though about two miles from my houfe, a
woman whofe daughter was fervant in the houfe

contiguous

contiguous to mine, came to her miftrefs, to entreat that fhe might be out of the way; and it was not without much difficulty that fhe was pacified, and prevailed upon to continue in the houfe, her miftrefs faying that fhe was as fafe as herfelf.

On feveral other occafions the neighbourhood has been greatly alarmed on account of my being fo near them. Nor was this without apparent reafon. I could name a perfon, and to appearance a reputable tradef-man, who, in the company of his friends, in the hearing of one of my late congregation at Birmingham, but without knowing him to be fuch, declared that, in cafe of any difturbance, they would immediately come to Hackney, evidently for the purpofe of mifchief. In this ftate of things, it is not to be wondered at, that of many fervants who were recommended to me, and fome that were actually hired, very few could, for a long time, be prevailed upon to live with me.

Thefe facts not only fhew how general was the idea of my particular infecurity in this country; but what is of much more confequence, and highly in-terefting to the country at large, an idea of the ge-neral difpofition to rioting and violence that prevails in it, and that the Diffenters are the objects of it. Mr. Pitt very juftly obferved, in his fpeech on the fubject of the riots in Birmingham, that it was " the " effervefcence of the public mind." Indeed the effervefcible matter has exifted in this country even fince the civil wars in the time of Charles I. and it was particularly apparent in the reign of queen Ann. But the power of government under the former princes

of

of the Houfe of Hanover prevented its doing any mifchief. The late events fhew that this power is no longer exerted as it ufed to be, but that, on the contrary, there prevails an idea, well or ill founded, that tumultuary proceedings againft Diffenters will not receive any effectual difcouragement. After what has taken place with refpect to Birmingham, all idea of much hazard for infulting and abufing the Diffenters is entirely vanifhed; whereas the difpofition to injure the Catholics was effectually checked by the proceedings of the year 1780. From that time *they* have been fafe, and I rejoice in it. But from the year 1791, the Diffenters have been more expofed to infult and outrage than ever.

Having fixed myfelf at Clapton; unhinged as I had been, and having loft the labour of feveral years; yet flattering myfelf that I fhould end my days here, I took a long leafe of my houfe, and expended a confiderable fum in improving it. I alfo determined, with the affiftance of my friends, to refume my philofophical and other purfuits; and after an interruption amounting to about two years, it was with a pleafure that I cannot defcribe, that I entered my new laboratory, and began the moft common preparatory proceffes, with a view to fome original inquiries. With what fuccefs I have laboured, the public has already in fome meafure feen, and may fee more hereafter.

But though I did not choofe (notwithftanding I found myfelf expofed to continual infult) to leave my native country, I found it neceffary to provide for &y fons elfewhere. My eldeft fon was fettled in a bufinefs, which promifed to be very advantageous, at Manchefter; but his partner, though a man of liberality himfelf, informed him, on perceiving the general prevalence of the fpirit which produced the riots in Birmingham, that, owing to his relationfhip to *me*, he was under the neceffity of propofing a feparation, which accordingly took place.

On this he had an invitation to join another connexion, in a bufinefs in which the fpirit of party could not have much affected him; but he declined it. And after he had been prefent at the affizes at Warwick, he conceived fuch an idea of this country, that I do not believe that any propofal, however advantageous, would have induced him to continue in it; fo much was he affected on perceiving his father treated as I had been.

Determining to go to America, where he had no profpect but that of being a farmer, he wifhed to fpend a fhort time with a perfon who has greatly diftinguifhed himfelf in that way, and one who from his own general principles, and his friendfhip for myfelf, would have given him the beft advice and affiftance in his power. He, however, declined it, and acknowledged fome time after, that had it been known, as it muft have been, to his landlord, that he had a fon of *mine* with him, he feared he fhould have been turned out of his farm.

My fecond fon, who was prefent both at the riot, and the affizes, felt more indignation ftill, and willingly liftened to a propofal to fettle in France; and there his reception was but too flattering. However,

on

on the breaking out of the war with this country, all mercantile profpects being fufpended, he wifhed to go to America. There his eldeft and youngeft brother have joined him, and they are now looking out for a fettlement, having as yet no fixed views.

The neceffity I was under of fending my fons out of this country, was my principal inducement to fend the little property that I had out of it too; fo that I had nothing in England befides my library, apparatus, and houfehold goods. By this, I felt myfelf greatly relieved, it being of little confequence where a man already turned fixty ends his days. Whatever good or evil I have been capable of, is now chiefly done; and I truft that the fame confcioufnefs of integrity, which has fupported me hitherto, will carry me through any thing that may yet be referved for me. Seeing, however, no great profpect of doing much good, or having much enjoyment, here, I am now preparing to follow my fons; hoping to be of fome ufe to them in their prefent unfettled ftate, and that Providence may yet, advancing in years as I am, find me fome fphere of ufefulnefs along with them.

As to the great odium that I have incurred, the charge of *fedition*, or my being an enemy to the conftitution or peace of my country, is a mere pretence for it; though it has been fo much urged, that it is now generally believed, and all attempts to undeceive the public with refpect to it avail nothing at all. The whole courfe of my ftudies, from early life, fhews how little *politics* of any kind have been my object. Indeed to have written fo much as I

have

have in *theology*, and to have done so much in *experimental philosophy*, and at the same time to have had my mind occupied, as it is supposed to have been, with factious politics, I must have had faculties more than human. Let any person only cast his eye over the long list of my publications, and he will see that they relate almost wholly to theology, philosophy, or general literature.

I did, however, when I was a younger man, and before it was in my power to give much attention to philosophical pursuits, write a small anonymous political pamphlet, on the *State of Liberty in this Country*, about the time of Mr. Wilkes's election for Middlesex, which gained me the acquaintance, and I may say the friendship, of Sir George Savile, and which I had the happiness to enjoy as long as he lived.

At the request also of Dr. Franklin and Dr. Fothergill, I wrote an address to the Dissenters on the subject of the approaching rupture with America, a pamphlet which Sir George Savile, and my other friends, circulated in great numbers, and it was thought with some effect.

After this I entirely ceased to write any thing on the subject of politics, except as far as the business of the *Test Act*, and of *Civil Establishments of Religion*, had a connexion with politics. And though, at the recommendation of Dr. Price, I was presently after this taken into the family of the Marquis of Lansdowne, and I entered into almost all his views, as thinking them just and liberal, I never wrote a single pamphlet,

pamphlet, or even a paragraph in a newfpaper, all
the time that I was with him, which was feven years.

I never preached a political fermon in my life, un-
lefs fuch as, I believe, all Diffenters ufually preach
on the fifth of November, in favour of *civil and religious liberty,* may be faid to be political. And on
thefe occafions, I am confident, that I never advanced any fentiment but fuch as, till of late years,
would have tended to recommend, rather than
render me obnoxious, to thofe who direct the admi-
niftration of this country. And the doctrines which
I adopted when young, and which were even popular
then (except with the clergy, who were at that time
generally difaffected to the family on the throne) I
cannot abandon, merely becaufe the times are fo
changed, that they are now become unpopular, and
the expreffion and communication of them hazardous.

Farther, though I by no means difapprove of
focieties for political information, fuch as are now
every where difcountenanced, and generally fup-
preffed, I never was a member of any of them; nor,
indeed, did I ever attend any public meeting, if I
could decently avoid it, owing to habits acquired in
ftudious and retired life.

From a miftake of my talents and difpofition, I
was invited by many of the departments in France,
to reprefent them in the prefent National Conven-
tion, after I had been made a citizen of France, on
account of my being confidered as one who had been
perfecuted for my attachment to the caufe of liberty
here. But though the invitation was repeated with

the moſt flattering importunity, I never heſitated about declining it.

I can farther ſay with reſpect to politics, concerning which I believe every Engliſhman has ſome opinion or other (and at preſent, owing to the peculiar nature of the preſent war, it is almoſt the only topic of general converſation) that, except in company, I hardly ever think of the ſubject, my reading, meditation, and writing, being almoſt wholly engroſſed by theology, and philoſophy; and of late, as for many years before the riots in Birmingham, I have ſpent a very great proportion of my time, as my friends well know, in my laboratory.

If, then, my real crime has not been *ſedition*, or *treaſon*, what has it been? For every *effect* muſt have ſome adequate *cauſe*, and therefore the odium that I have incurred muſt have been owing to ſomething in my declared ſentiments, or conduct, that has expoſed me to it. In my own opinion, it cannot have been any thing but my open hoſtility to the doctrines of the eſtabliſhed church, and more eſpecially to all civil eſtabliſhments of religion whatever. This has brought upon me the implacable reſentment of the great body of the clergy; and they have found other methods of oppoſing me beſides *argument*, and that uſe of the *preſs* which is equally open to us all. They have alſo found an able ally and champion in Mr. Burke, who (without any provocation except that of anſwering his book on the French Revolution) has taken ſeveral opportunities of inveighing againſt me, in a place where he knows

I cannot

I cannot reply to him, and from which he also knows that his accusation will reach every corner of the country, and consequently thousands of persons, who will never read any writings of mine*. They have had another, and still more effectual vehicle of their abuse in what are called the *treasury news-papers*, and other popular publications.

By these and other means, the same party spirit which was the cause of the riots in Birmingham, has been increasing ever since, especially in that neighbourhood; a remarkable instance of which may be seen in a *Letter* addressed, but not sent, to me from *Mr. Foley, rector of Stourbridge*, who acknowledges the satisfaction that he and his brethren have received from one of the grossest and coarsest pieces of abuse of me that has yet appeared, which, as a curious specimen of the kind, I inserted in the *Appendix of my Appeal*, and in which I am represented as no better than Guy Fawkes, or the devil himself. This very Christian divine recommends to the members of the established church to decline all commercial dealings with Dissenters, as an effectual method of exterminating them. *Defoe's Shortest Way with the*

---

* Mr. Burke having said in the House of Commons, that "I was made a citizen of France on account of my declared "hostility to the constitution of this country," I, in the public papers, denied the charge, and called upon him for the proofs of it. As he made no reply, in the preface to my F.st Sermon of the last year, I said, p. 9, that "it sufficiently appeared that he "had neither ability to maintain his charge, nor virtue to retract "it." A year more of silence on his part having now elapsed, this is become more evident than before.

Dissenters,

Diffenters*, would have taught him a more effectual method ftill. And yet this Mr. Foley, whom I never faw, and who could not have had any particular caufe of enmity to me, had, like Mr. Madan of Birmingham, a chara&er for liberality. What, then, have we to expe& from others, when we find fo much bigotry and rancour in fuch men as thefe?

Many times, by the encouragement of perfons from whom better things might have been expe&ed, I have been burned in effigy along with Mr. Paine; and numberlefs infulting and threatening letters have been fent to me from all parts of the kingdom. It is not poffible for any man to have condu&ed himfelf more peaceably than I have done all the time that I have lived at Clapton, yet it has not exempted me not only from the worft fufpicions, but very grofs infults. A very friendly and innocent club, which I found in the place, has been confidered as *Jacoline* chiefly on my account; and at one time there was caufe of apprehenfion that I fhould have been brought into danger for lending one of Mr. Paine's books. But with fome difficulty the neighbourhood was fatisfied that I was innocent.

As nothing had been paid to me on account of damages in the riot, when I publifhed the fecond part of my *Appeal* to the public on the fubje&, it may be proper to fay, that it was paid fome time in the beginning of the year 1793, with intereft only from the firft of January of the fame year, though the injury was received in July, 1791; when equity

* A tra& written in a grave ironical ftile, advifing to hang them all.

evidently

evidently required, that it ought to have been allowed from the time of the riot, efpecially as, in all the
cafes, the allowance was far fhort of the lofs. In my
cafe it fell fhort, as I have fhewn, not lefs than two
thoufand pounds. And the loffes fuftained by the other
fufferers far exceeded mine. Public juftice alfo required that, if the forms of law, local enmity, or any
other caufe, had prevented our receiving full indem-
nification, it fhould have been made up to us from
the public treafury; the great end of all civil government being protection from violence, or an indemni-
fication for it. Whatever we might in equity claim,
the country owes us, and, if it be juft, will fome time
or other pay, and with intereft.

I would farther obferve, that fince, in a variety of
cafes, money is allowed where the injury is not of a
pecuniary nature, merely becaufe no other compen-
fation can be given, the fame fhould have been done
with refpect to me, on account of the deftruction of
my manufcripts, the interruption of my purfuits, the
lofs of a pleafing and advantageous fituation, &c.
&c. and had the injury been fuftained by a *clergy-
man*, he would, I doubt not, have claimed, and been
allowed, very large damages on this account. So
far, however, was there any idea of the kind in *my*
favour, that my counfel advifed me to make no
mention of my manufcript *Lectures on the Conftitution
and Laws of England*, a work about as large as that
of Blackftone (as may be feen by the fyllabus of the
particular lectures, fixty-three in all, publifhed in the
firft edition of my *Effay on a Courfe of liberal Educa-*
tion

tion for civil and active Life) becaufe it would be taken for granted that they were of feditious nature, and would therefore have been of differvice to me with the jury. Accordingly they were, in the account of my loffes, included in the article of fo much *paper*. After thefe loffes, had I had nothing but the juftice of my country to look to, I muft have funk under the burden, incapable of any farther exertions. It was the feafonable generofity of my friends that prevented this, and put it in my power, though with the unavoidable lofs of near two years, to refume my former purfuits.

A farther proof of the exceffive bigotry of this country is, that, though the clergy of Birmingham, refenting what I advanced in the firft part of my *Appeal*, replied to it, and pledged themfelves to go through with the enquiry along with me, till the whole truth fhould be inveftigated, they have made no reply to the *Second Part of my Appeal*, in which I brought fpecific charges againft themfelves, and other perfons by name, proving them to have been the promoters and abettors of the riot; and yet they have as much refpect fhewn to them as ever, and the country at large pays no attention to it. Had the clergy been the injured perfons, and Diffenters the rioters, unable to anfwer the charges brought againft them, fo great would have been the general indignation at their conduct, that I am perfuaded it would not have been poffible for them to continue in the country.

I could, if I were fo difpofed, give my readers

many

many more inſtances of the bigotry of the clergy of the church of England with reſpect to me, which could not fail to excite, in generous minds, equal indignation and contempt; but I forbear. Had I, however, foreſeen what I am now witneſs to, I certainly ſhould not have made any attempt to replace my library or apparatus, and I ſoon repented of having done it. But this being done, I was willing to make ſome uſe of both before another interruption of my purſuits. I began to philoſophize, and make experiments, rather late in life, being near forty, for want of the neceſſary means of doing any thing in this way; and my purſuits have been much interrupted by removals (never indeed choſen by myſelf, but rendered neceſſary by circumſtances) and my time being now ſhort, I hoped to have had no occaſion for more than one, and that a final, remove. But the circumſtances above mentioned have induced me, though with great and ſincere regret, to undertake another, and to a greater diſtance than any that I have hitherto made.

I profeſs not to be unmoved by the aſpect of things exhibited in this Diſcourſe. But notwithſtanding this, I ſhould willingly have awaited my fate in my native country, whatever it had been, if I had not had ſons in America, and if I did not think that a field of public uſefulneſs, which is evidently cloſing upon me here, might open to more advantage there.

I alſo own that I am not unaffected by ſuch unexampled puniſhments as thoſe of Mr. Muir and my

b   friend

friend Mr. Palmer, for offences, which, if, in the
eye of reason, they be any at all, are flight, and very
infufficiently proved; a meafure fo fubverfive of that
freedom of fpeaking and acting, which has hitherto
been the great pride of Britons. But the fentence of
Mr. Winterbotham, for delivering from the pulpit
what I am perfuaded he never did deliver, and
which, fimilar evidence might have drawn upon myfelf, or any other diffenting minifter, who was an
object of general diflike, has fomething in it ftill
more alarming*. But I truft that confcious inno-

cence

---

* I truft that the friends of liberty, efpecially among the Diffenters, will not fail to do every thing in their power to make
Mr. Winterbottom's confinement, and alfo the fufferings of Mr.
Palmer and his companions, as eafy to them as poffible. Having
been affifted in a feafon of perfecution myfelf, I fhould be very ill
deferving of the favours I have received, if I was not particularly
defirous of recommending fuch cafes as theirs to general confideration. Here difference in religious fentiment is leaft of all
to be attended to. On the contrary, let thofe who in this refpect
differ the moft from Mr. Winterbottom, which is my own cafe,
exert themfelves the moft in his favour. When men of unquef-
tionable integrity and piety fuffer in confequence of acting (as
fuch perfons always will do) from a principle of *confcience*, they
muft command the refpect even of their enemies, if they alfo act
from principle, though they be thereby led to proceed in an op-
pofite direction.

The cafe of men of education and reflection (and who act from
the beft intentions with refpect to the community) committing
what only *ftate policy* requires to be confidered as *crimes*, but
which are allowed on all hands to imply no moral turpitude, fo
as to render them unfit for heaven and happinefs hereafter, is not
to be confounded with that of common felons. There was nothing in the conduct of Louis XIV. and his minifters, that appeared fo fhocking, fo contrary to all ideas of juftice, humanity
and decency, and that has contributed more to render their me-

mory

cence would support me as it does him, under whatever prejudiced and violent men might *do* to me, as well as *say* of me. But I see no occasion to expose myself to danger without any prospect of doing good, or to continue any longer in a country in which I am so unjustly become the object of general dislike, and not retire to another, where I have reason to think I shall be better received. And I trust that the same good Providence which has attended me hitherto, and made me happy in my present situation, and all my former ones, will attend and bless me in what may still be before me. In all events, *The will of God be done.*

I cannot refrain from repeating again, that I leave my native country with real regret, never expecting to find any where else society so suited to my disposition and habits, such friends as I have here (whose attachment has been more than a balance to all the abuse I have met with from others) and especially to replace one particular Christian friend, in whose absence I shall, for some time at least, find all the world a blank. Still less can I expect to resume my favourite pursuits, with any thing like the advantages I enjoy here. In leaving this country I also abandon a source of maintenance, which I can but ill bear to lose. I can, however, truly say, that I

mory execrated, than sending such men as Mr. Marolles, and other eminent Proteftants, who are now revered as faints and martyrs, to the gallies, along with the vileft mifcreants, Compared with this, the punifhment of death would be mercy. I truft that, in time, the Scots in general will think thefe meafures a difgrace to their country.

leave

leave it without any refentment, or ill will. On the contrary, I fincerely wifh my countrymen all happinefs; and when the time for reflection (which my abfence may accelerate) fhall come, my countrymen, I am confident, will do me more juftice. They will be convinced that every fufpicion they have been led to entertain to my difadvantage has been ill founded, and that I have even fome claims to their gratitude and efteem. In this cafe, I fhall look with fatisfaction to the time when, if my life be prolonged, I may vifit my friends in this country; and perhaps I may, notwithftanding my removal for the prefent, find a grave (as I believe is naturally the wifh of every man) in the land that gave me birth.

FAST

FAST SERMON,

February 28, 1794.

REPENT YE, FOR THE KINGDOM OF HEAVEN IS AT
HAND!   MATT. iii. 2.

Tʜɪs was the great burden of the preaching of
both John the Baptiſt and of our Saviour. But as
that *kingdom of heaven*, the approach of which they
announced, and which, by our Saviour's direction, is
the ſubject of our daily prayers, is not yet come,
but much nearer than it was in their time, there
muſt be a greater propriety in urging this exhorta-
tion at preſent, than there has ever yet been. It is
nothing but repentance that can prepare ſinful men
(and all men are more or leſs ſinners) to derive any
advantage from this kingdom, in which Chriſt and
the ſaints ſhall bear rule; that new ſtate of the
heavens and of the earth, in which *righteouſneſs* only
will dwell. And being a ſecond time called upon
by our rulers to humble ourſelves before God, on
account of the calamities we already feel, and thoſe
that we have reaſon to fear, and repentance being

B   the

the only means of averting his anger, and procuring
a ceſſation, or mitigation, of his heavy judgments, I
ſhall take this opportunity of urging it, from that
very critical and truly alarming ſituation, in which
almoſt the whole of Europe now finds itſelf, and this
country of ours, as having moſt at ſtake, perhaps
more than any other.

If we can learn any thing concerning what is before us, from the language of prophecy, great calamities, ſuch as the world has never yet experi-
enced, will precede that happy ſtate of things, in
which ' the kingdoms of this world will become the
' kingdom of our Lord Jeſus Chriſt;' and theſe calamities will chiefly affect thoſe nations which have
been the ſeat of the great antichriſtian power; or, as
all Proteſtants, and I believe juſtly, ſuppoſe, have
been ſubject to the ſee of Rome.   And it appears to
me highly probable, as I hinted in my laſt diſcourſe
✓ on this occaſion, that the preſent diſturbances in
Europe are the beginning of thoſe very calamitous
times.   I therefore think there is a call for unuſual
ſeriouſneſs, and attention to the courſe of Divine
Providence, that when ' the judgments of God are
' abroad in the earth, the inhabitants thereof may
' learn righteouſneſs,' ſo as to be prepared for whatever events the now rapid wheels of time may diſ-
cloſe.   Let us then, my brethren, make a ſerious
pauſe.   Let us look back to the antient prophecies,
and compare them with the preſent ſtate of things
around us; and let us then look to ourſelves, to our

own

own fentiments and conduct, that we may feel and act as our peculiar circumftances require.

The future happy ftate of the world, when the Jews fhall be reftored to their own country, and be at the head of all the nations of the earth, was firft diftinctly mentioned by Ifaiah, and other prophets who were nearly cotemporary with him; but it was firft denominated *the kingdom of heaven*, and announced as to be adminiftered by *the Son of Man*, or *the Meffiab*, by Daniel. It was, however, by other prophets, given to a defcendant of David. All Chriftians confider Jefus as this defcendant of David, or the promifed Meffiah. The miftake which the ✓ Jews were under, arofe from their wholly overlook-, ing the fuffering ftate of the Meffiah, and imagining that his *firft* coming would be that mentioned by Daniel, *in the clouds of heaven*; and confequently that his kingdom would commence on his firft appearance.

Jefus, knowing himfelf to be the Meffiah, never denied that, at a proper time, he would appear as a king; nor could there have been at that time any uncertainty about the meaning of the term *king*. When Pilate afked Jefus if he was a king, he acknowledged it, and added that he was fent to bear witnefs to *that*, as well as to other truths; though, to obviate the jealoufy of Pilate, and the Roman government, he faid that his kingdom was *not of this world*; fo that it did not interfere with the governments which then exifted in the world, being that

kingdom

kingdom of heaven which was to take place hereafter, and to be exerciſed· upon maxims very different from thoſe of the then exiſting·kingdoms.

Jeſus alſo ſaid that, when he ſhould reign, his apoſtles would reign with him, and that they ſhould ' ſit upon twelve thrones, judging the twelve tribes ' of Iſrael.' Paul alſo ſaid, that ' the ſaints ſhall ' judge the world.' And it is remarkable that, in the original prophecy of Daniel, the adminiſtration of this kingdom of heaven is not ſaid to be wholly confined to one perſon, but to be extended to many, Dan. vii. 18. ' The ſaints of the Moſt High ſhall ' take the kingdom, and poſſeſs the kingdom for ' ever, even for ever and ever;' ver. 27. ' And the ' kingdom, and dominion, and the greatneſs of the ' 'kingdom, under the whole heaven, ſhall be given ' to the people of the ſaints of the Moſt High, whoſe ' kingdom is an everlaſting kingdom, and all do- ' minions ſhall ſerve, and obey him,' or rather, ' obey *it*.'

That this will be a proper *kingdom*, though a kingdom of righteouſneſs, the object of which will be the happineſs of the ſubjects of it, is farther evident from the other kingdoms which are to be overthrown in order to make way for it. For had it been that purely *ſpiritual kingdom* which ſome ſuppoſe, what occaſion was there for the deſtruction of the other kingdoms; ſince they would not have interfered with it, but might have ſubſiſted at the ſame time?

In

In the firft vifion of Nebuchadnezzar, interpreted by Daniel, this future kingdom of heaven is reprefented by ' a little ftone, cut out of a mountain with-
' out hands,' which *fmote* the image reprefenting the preceding kingdoms, Dan. ii. 34. and ' brake it to
' pieces,' when itfelf ' became a great mountain,
' filling the whole earth.' In the interpretation of this vifion, ver. 44, it is faid, ' In the days of thefe
' kings fhall the God of heaven fet up a kingdom
' which fhall never be deftroyed, and the kingdom
' fhall not be left to other people, but it fhall break .
' in pieces, and confume all thefe kingdoms, and it
' fhall ftand for ever;' evidently in the place of the other kingdoms. It is, therefore, an inftitution adapted to anfwer the purpofe of them, but in a much better manner.

This kingdom, however, a kingdom of truth and righteoufnefs, will not be eftablifhed without the greateft convulfions, and the violent overthrow of other kingdoms. Every defcription, figurative or otherwife, of this great revolution, clearly implies √ violence, and confequently great calamity. The little ftone *fmiting* the image, and *breaking it in pieces*, is far from giving an idea of a peaceable revolution, but one that will be effected with great violence, and in a fhort time. The following language is peculiarly emphatical. ' Then was the iron, the clay,
' the brafs, the filver, and the gold,' (all the materials of which the image confifted) ' broken to pieces
' together, and became as the chaff of the fummer

B 3 ' floor,

' floor, and the wind carried them away, and no
' place was found for them; and the ſtone that
' ſmote the image became a great mountain, and
' filled the whole earth.'   In the interpretation it is
ſaid, ver. 44, ' that this new kingdom ſhall break in
' pieces, and cònſume all the other kingdoms.'

The ſame awful concluſion may be drawn from
the language uſed in the correſponding viſion of
Daniel himſelf, in the firſt year of Belſhazzar, in
which the four great empires, which in Nebuchadnezzar's dream had been repreſented by the *four
metals,* of which the image that he ſaw conſiſted,
are repreſented by *four beaſts,* and the laſt of them is
ſaid (Dan. vii. 11) not to die a natural death, but
to be ſlain, and moreover, his *body deſtroyed, and given
to the burning flame.*   As, in the former viſion, the
ten kingdoms, into which the laſt, or the Roman
empire was to be divided, were repreſented by the
ten toes of the image; in this viſion of Daniel they
are repreſented by the ten horns of the laſt beaſt.
Theſe are ſaid to be ten kingdoms, or thrones, and
theſe thrones are ſaid to be *caſt down,* Dan. vii. 9.
clearly implying violence in their diſſolution.

In the language of prophecy, great, and eſpecially
ſudden revolutions, in kingdoms and ſtates, are frequently repreſented by *earthquakes;* and alſo the
ſupreme powers on earth by the ſun, moon, and ſtars.
And, in agreement with the preceding view, ſug-
geſted by Daniel, the prophet Haggai, who wrote
after him, to comfort his countrymen in their low
                                                    and

and diftreffed circumftances, and gloomy profpects, when they were erecting a poor and contemptible temple, compared with that of Solomon, affures them, that the glory of the *latter houfe*, meaning, I am perfuaded, not the houfe they were then building, for that was taken down by Herod; nor yet that of Herod, but the *laft* houfe, the glorious temple defcribed by Ezekiel, as to be built after the return of the Jews to their own country, fhould be greater than that of the former houfe built by Solomon. Haggai defcribes the great revolution that is to precede it in the following manner. Hag. ii. 6. ' For thus faith the Lord of Hofts, Yet once it is a ' little while, and I will fhake the heavens and the ' earth, and the fea, and the dry land, and I will ' fhake all nations, and the defire of all nations fhall ' come, and I will fill this houfe with glory, faith the ' Lord of Hofts. The glory of this latter houfe fhall ' be greater than that of the former, faith the Lord ' of Hofts; and in this place will I give peace, faith ' the Lord of Hofts.' What can be this *peace*, but the future peaceful and happy ftate of the world under the Meffiah? and what can be this *fhaking of the nations*, that is to precede it, but great convulfions, and fudden revolutions, fuch as we fee now beginning to take place?

The laft great power that is foretold, as to arife among the ten kingdoms into which the Roman empire is to be divided, is reprefented by the *little horn*, which is faid to arife after the ten, fignifying, I

doubt not, the Papal power. It is ſaid, Dan. vii. 20,
' to have eyes, and a mouth that ſpake very great
' things, whoſe look was more ſtout than his fellows,
' which made war with the ſaints, and prevailed
' againſt them, until the antient of days came, and
'judgment was given to the ſaints of the Moſt High,
' and the time came that the ſaints poſſeſſed the
' kingdom.' This power, in the interpretation of
the viſion, is ſaid to be one that ſhould ' ſpeak great
' words againſt the Moſt High, and to wear out the
' ſaints of the Moſt High, and to think to change
' times and laws.' It is added, ' They ſhall be given
' into his hand until a time, and times, and the di-
' viding of time,' the very period for the duration
of the great antichriſtian power in the Revelation.

When the termination of this laſt power is deſcribed, it is ſaid, ver. 26, ' The judgment ſhall ſit,
' and they ſhall take away his dominion, to conſume
' and to deſtroy it unto the end,' which clearly implies nothing of a peaceable nature, but ſomething
exceedingly violent and calamitous.

This is, no doubt, the ſame awful period that is
ſpoken of in the laſt chapter of Daniel, ch. xii. ver. 1.
' And at that time ſhall Michael ſtand up, the great
' prince which ſtandeth for the children of thy peo-
' ple, and there ſhall be a time of trouble, ſuch as
' never was ſince there was a nation, even to that
' ſame time; and at that time thy people ſhall be
' delivered, every one that ſhall be found written in
' the book. And many of them that ſleep in the
' duſt

' duft of the earth fhall awake.' For that the refur-
furrection, at leaft in part, will take place at the
commencement of this great period, is agreeable to
the uniform language of fcripture on the fubject.

All the prophecies in the New Teftament concerning the fall of Antichrift, and the commencement
of the proper kingdom of heaven, and of Chrift, exactly correfpond with thofe which I have quoted from
the Old Teftament. The fecond coming of Chrift is
reprefented by the apoftle Paul, 2 Thef. i. 7, as an
event exceedingly awful, and dreadful to the wicked.
' He will be revealed from heaven, with his mighty
' angels, in flaming fire, taking vengeance on them
' that know not God.'

That the great antichriftian power is to be deftroyed at this fecond coming of Chrift, and not properly before, and therefore that its final deftruction
will be fudden, is evident from what the fame apoftle
fays afterwards, 2 Thef. ii. 8. ' Then fhall that wicked
' one be revealed, whom the Lord fhall confume
' with the fpirit of his mouth, and fhall deftroy with
' the brightnefs of his coming, even him whofe
' coming is after the working of Satan, with all
' power, and figns, and lying wonders, and with all
' deceivablenefs of unrighteoufnefs, in them that
' perifh;' characters fufficiently evident of the church
of Rome.

The account that is given, in the book of Revelation, of the commencement of the laft great period, fignified by the blowing of the *feventh trumpet*,
when

when the kingdoms of the earth are to become the
kingdoms of our Lord Jeſus Chriſt, Rev. ii. 15, is
immediately preceded by the third, and probably far
the greateſt of the *three woes*, the firſt of which was
occaſioned by the conqueſts of the Saracens, and the
ſecond by thoſe of the Turks, as the order of the
events deſcribed under the preceding trumpets evidently implies.   And the ſtate of things at this time
is deſcribed in the following emphatical language of
the four and twenty elders, who are ſaid, on this occaſion, to fall on their faces, and to worſhip God,
Rev. xi. 17. ' We give thee thanks, O Lord God
' Almighty, who art, and waſt, and art to come, be-
' cauſe thou haſt taken to thee thy great power and
' haſt reigned. And the nations were angry, and thy
' wrath is come, and the time of the dead that they
' muſt be judged, and that thou ſhouldeſt give re-
' ward to thy ſervants the prophets, and ſhouldeſt
' deſtroy them that deſtroy the earth *.'

We have here a wonderful concurrence of great
events, and among theſe is the *anger of the nations*,
followed by the *deſtruction of them that have deſtroyed
the earth*.   Now how has the earth been deſtroyed
by the men who *have* deſtroyed it, but by deſolating
wars, and the deſtruction that has thereby been made
of mankind?   In like manner, then, may we con-

* On this ſubject I refer my readers to two ſermons lately
publiſhed by the Rev. Elkanan Wincheſter, entitled *The Three
Woe Trumpets*, deſerving the ſerious conſideration of all Chriſtians,
who are attentive to the *ſigns of the times*.

clude

clude that thofe deftructive powers will themfelves
be deftroyed, probably by one another, in thofe *wars*
which the apoftle James fays arife from *men's lufts*,
the luft of ambition and revenge. And when, my
brethren, have we feen, or heard of, fuch anger and
rage in nations, fuch violence in carrying on war,
and fuch deftruction of men, as at this very time?
It is thought that the laft campaign only has deftroyed many more men than all the eight years of
the American war, and probably more than the long
war before it; and from the increafed armaments of
the belligerent powers, and their increafing animo-
fity, it is probable that the approaching campaign
will be more bloody than the laft.

What has more eminently contributed to deftroy
the earth, than the antichriftian and idolatrous ecclefiaftical eftablifhments of Chriftianity, that have
fubfifted in thefe weftern parts of the world; many
more perfons having been deftroyed by Chriftians,
as they have called themfelves, than by Heathens?
And do we not fee one, and one of the principal, of
thofe eftablifhments already, and completely, deftroyed?

A more highly wrought picture of the deftruction and flaughter of men, that will precede this glorious period in which ' God will take to himfelf his
' great power and reign,' we find in the 19th chapter of the Revelation, which defcribes the triumph
of the faints on the occafion. 'After thefe things I
' heard a great voice of much people in heaven,
' faying,

' ſaying, Alleluia, Salvation, and glory, and honour,
' and power, unto the Lord our God; for true and
' right are his judgments. For he hath judged the
' great whore, which did corrupt the earth with her
' fornication, and hath avenged the blood of his ſer-
' vants at her hand.' That this has a connexion with
the ſecond coming of Chriſt, appears from what immediately follows, ver. 11. 'And I ſaw heaven open-
' ed, and behold a white horſe, and he that ſat upon
' him was called faithful and true, and in righteouſ-
' neſs he ſhall judge and make war. His eyes were
' as a flame of fire, and on his head were many
' crowns, and he had a name written which no man
' knew but he himſelf. And he was clothed in a
' veſture dipped in blood, and his name is called
' THE WORD OF GOD. And the armies which were
' in heaven followed him upon white horſes, clothed
' in fine linen, white and clean; and out of his mouth
' goeth a ſharp ſword, that with it he ſhould ſmite
' the nations; and he ſhall rule them with a rod of
' iron, and he treadeth the wine-preſs of the fierce-
' neſs of the wrath of Almighty God. And he hath
' on his veſture, and on his thigh, a name written,
' KING OF KINGS AND LORD OF LORDS.'

That there will be literally great ſlaughter of
men on the occaſion, is clearly indicated in what
follows, figurative and hyperbolical as the language
is, ver. 17. 'And I ſaw an angel ſtanding in the ſun,
' and he cried with a loud voice, ſaying to all the
' fowls that fly in the midſt of heaven, Come and
' gather

' gather yourfelves together, unto the fupper of the
' great God, that ye may eat the flefh of kings, and
' the flefh of captains, and the flefh of mighty men,
' and the flefh of horfes, and them that fit on them,
' and the flefh of all men, both free and bond, both
' fmall and great.'

The fame is evident from the account of the
pouring out of the third vial, Rev. xvi. 14, &c.
' And the third angel poured out his vial on the ri-
' vers and fountains of water, and they became
' blood. And I heard the angel of the waters fay,
' Thou art righteous, O Lord, who art, and waft,
' and fhalt be, becaufe thou haft judged thus. For
' they have fhed the blood of faints and prophets,
' and thou haft given them blood to drink, for they
' are worthy.'

That this great flaughter will be made on the deftruction of the antichriftian power, called in this
book *the beaft*, fupported by *the kings of the earth*, is
evident from the next verfes, ver. 19. ' And I faw
' the beaft, and the kings of the earth, and their
' armies, gathered together, to make war againft him
' that fat on the horfe, and againft his army. And
' the beaft was taken, and with him the falfe pro-
' phet, that wrought miracles before him, with which
' he deceived them that had received the mark of
' the beaft, and them that worfhipped his image.
' Thefe were both caft alive into a lake of fire
' burning with brimftone. And the remnant were
' flain with the fword of him that fat upon the horfe,
' which

' which ſword proceeded out of his mouth, and all
' the fowls were filled with their fleſh.'

After this follows the deſcription of the millennium,
chap. xx. ver. 4. ' And I ſaw thrones, and they ſat
' upon them, and judgment was given unto them;
' and I ſaw the ſouls of them that were beheaded
' for the witneſs of Jeſus, and for the word of God,
' and which had not worſhipped the beaſt, neither
' his image, neither had received his mark upon
' their forehead, or in their hands, and they lived and
' reigned with Chriſt a thouſand years. But the reſt
' of the dead lived not again until the thouſand years
' were finiſhed. This is the firſt reſurrection. Bleſſ-
' ed and holy is he that hath part in the firſt reſur-
' rection. On ſuch the ſecond death hath no power,
' but they ſhall be prieſts of God, and of Chriſt,
' and they ſhall reign with him a thouſand
' years.'

To me it appears not improbable, that ſeveral
circumſtances in our Saviour's prophecy concerning
the deſtruction of Jeruſalem, and the deſolation of
Judea, relate to this great and more diſtant period.
For it was delivered in anſwer to a queſtion put to
him by his diſciples, which reſpected both the events,
on the idea of their being coincident. ' Tell us,' ſay
they, Matt. xxiv. 3, ' when ſhall theſe things be,
' and what ſhall be the ſign of thy coming, and of
' the end of the age.' In anſwer to this, he ſays,
firſt, as it is in Luke, whoſe account in this caſe
ſeems to be the moſt orderly and diſtinct of any,

chap.

chap. xxi. ver. 9. ' But when ye fhall hear of wars,
' and commotions, be not terrified; for thefe things
' muft firft come to pafs, but the end is not by and
' by. Then faid he unto them, Nation fhall rife
' againft nation, and kingdom againft kingdom, and
' great earthquakes fhall be in divers places, and fa-
' mines, and peftilences, and fearful fights, and great
' figns·fhall there be from heaven. But before all
' thefe they fhall lay their hands on you, and perfe-
' cute you, delivering you up to the fynagogues, and
' into prifons, being brought before kings and rulers
' for my name's fake.'

I am the more inclined to think that fome things
in this prediction have this farther reference, becaufe
in them Jefus exprefsly quotes the language of Daniel recited above, which unqueftionably has this
reference; as when he fays, Matt. xxix. 20. ' There
' fhall be great tribulation, fuch as was not fince the
' beginning of the world to this time, no nor ever
' fhall be: And except thofe days fhould be fhort-
' ened, there fhould no flefh be faved, but for the
' elect's fake thofe days fhall be fhortened.'

It feems ftill more evident that this prediction ad-
mits of this interpretation, from what follows, which
exactly correfponds to the more antient prophecies.
Mat. xxiv. 29. ' Immediately after the tribulation of
' thofe days fhall the fun be darkened, and the moon
' not give her light, and the ftars fhall fall from
' heaven, and the powers of the heavens fhall be
'fhaken;' which are almoft the very words of the

prophet

prophet Haggai quoted above. ' And then ſhall ap-
' pear the ſign of the Son of Man in heaven. And
' then ſhall all the tribes of the earth mourn. And
' they ſhall ſee the Son of Man coming in the clouds
' of heaven, with power and great glory. And he
' ſhall ſend his angels with a great ſound of a trumpet,
' and they ſhall gather together his elect, from the
' four winds, from one end of heaven to the other.'

That this great tribulation was a diſtant event,
and did not reſpect the Jews, but the Gentiles, is
probable from Jeſus calling it, Luke xxi. 25, ' the
' diſtreſs of nations,' or ' the nations,' i. e. the ' Gen-
' tiles,' ' men's hearts,' he ſubjoins, ' failing them for
' fear, and for looking after thoſe things which are
' coming on the earth. For the powers of heaven
' ſhall be ſhaken,' that is, there will be great convul-
ſions, and violent revolutions, in kingdoms and
ſtates; ' And then ſhall they ſee the Son of Man
' coming in clouds, with power and great glory.'

That this tribulation is coincident with that which
is to precede the reſtoration of the Jews, is probable
from his ſaying immediately before, ver. 24, ' Jeru-
' ſalem ſhall be trodden down of the Gentiles, till the
' times of the Gentiles be fulfilled,' that is, till it ſhall
come to be their turn to be puniſhed; the deſtruction of the Gentiles, who had oppreſſed the Jews,
commencing with the reſtoration of that highly fa-
voured nation.

Jeſus farther ſays, Luke xxi. 22. ' Theſe be the
' days of vengeance, that all the things which are
' written

' written may be fulfilled.' Now the only days of
vengeance particularly announced by the antient
prophets, to which Jefus here alludes, relate to
the judgments of God upon the Gentiles who had
fhewn enmity to the Jews, and efpecially in their op-
pofition to their re-fettlement in their own country.

There is nothing more clear in the whole compafs
of prophecy, as I have fhewn on another occafion,
than that after the deftined period for the difperfion
and calamities of the Jews, the heavieft of all the divine judgments will fall upon thofe nations by whom
they fhall have been oppreffed; and this will involve
almoft all the nations of the world, but more efpecially thofe of thefe weftern parts, which have been
fubject firft to the Roman empire, and then to the
fee of Rome.

Mofes fays, Deut. xxx. 7. ' The Lord thy God
' will put all thefe curfes' (thofe which were threat-
ened to fall upon them) ' upon thine enemies, and
' upon them that hate thee, and perfecute thee.' Ifa.
xliii. 25. ' I will contend with them that contend
' with thee, and I will fave thy children. And I will
' feed them that opprefs thee with their own flefh,
' and they fhall be drunken with their own blood,
' as with fweet wine, and all flefh fhall know that I,
' Jehovah, am thy Saviour, and thy Redeemer, the
' Mighty One of Jacob.' Zeph. iii. 19. ' Behold
' at that time I will undo all that afflict thee.' Jer.
xxx. 11. ' Though I make a full end of all the na-
' tions whither I have fcattered thee, yet will I not
C ' make

' make a full end of thee, but I will correct thee in
' meaſure.' Ezekiel, ſpeaking of the happy times
that will take place on the reſtoration of the Jews,
ſays, chap. xxviii. ver. 26. ' Yea they ſhall dwell
' with confidence, when I have executed judgments
' upon all thoſe that deſpiſe them round about them,
' and they ſhall know that I am Jehovah their God.'
Laſtly, Zechariah ſays, chap. xii. ver. 9. ' It ſhall
' come to paſs in that day, that I will ſeek to deſtroy
' all the nations that come againſt Jeruſalem.'

That there is to be a day of viſitation for all the
nations in this part of the world (all of whom have
diſtinguiſhed themſelves ſo by their oppreſſion and
maſſacre of the Jews) will now, I preſume, be ſufficiently apparent, if there be any truth in prophecy.
You will therefore naturally aſk, if there be any
ground for thinking, that thoſe judgments are now
about to take place; if ſo, how long they will probably continue, and when will be the commencement
of the glorious and happy times that are to follow.

That thoſe great troubles, ſo frequently mentioned in the antient prophecies, are now commencing,
I do own I ſtrongly ſuſpect, as I intimated the laſt
time that I addreſſed you on this occaſion; and the
events of the laſt year have contributed to ſtrengthen
that ſuſpicion; the ſtorm, however, may ſtill blow
over for the preſent, and the great ſcene of calamity
be reſerved for ſome future time, though I cannot
think it will be deferred long.

As to the preciſe time when the ſcene of calamity
will

will terminate, and the proper kingdom of Chrift will commence, he himfelf did not know, either before his death and refurrection, or afterwards. When he was queftioned on the fubject, he exprefsly faid, Mark xiii. 32, ' But of that day, and that hour, ' knoweth no man, no not the angels which are in ' heaven, neither the Son, but the Father.' When, after his refurrection, the difciples afked him, faying, Acts i. 6, ' Lord, wilt thou at this time reftore again ' the kingdom to Ifrael ?' he replied, ' It is not for ' you to know the times or the feafons, which the ' Father hath put in his own power.' It is enough for us to know the certainty of thefe great events, that our faith may not fail on the approach of the predicted calamity, confident that it will have the happieft iffue in God's own time. For the fame Being who foretold the evil which we fhall fee come to pafs, has likewife foretold the good that is to follow it.

That the fecond coming of Chrift will be coincident with the commencement of the millennium, or the future peaceable and happy ftate of the world (which, according to all the prophecies, will take place after the reftoration of the Jews) is evident from what Peter faid, in his addrefs to the Jews, on the occafion of his healing the lame man at the gate of the temple, Acts iii. 19. ' Repent ye, therefore, ' and be converted, that your fins may be blotted ' out, when the times of refrefhing fhall come from ' the prefence of the Lord. And he fhall fend Jefus

' Chrift,

' Chriſt, who before was preached unto you, whom
' the heavens muſt receive until the times of the
' reſtitution of all things, which God hath ſpoken by
' the mouth of all his holy prophets ſince the world
' began.' Now nothing is more evident than that
the only period that can be called the time of the
reſtitution of all things, or the paradiſiacal and happy
ſtate of the world, foretold by the antient prophets,
will follow the reſtoration of the Jews to their own
country. This, and nothing elſe, is the great burden
of all antient prophecy.

That this will be a joyful event to the Jewiſh
nation, when they will be convinced, perhaps by his
perſonal appearance among them, that he is their
promiſed Meſſiah, actually coming in the clouds of
heaven, appears from what our Saviour himſelf ſays,
Mat. xxi. 9. Luke xiii. 35. ' Verily I ſay unto you,
' ye ſhall not ſee me until the time come when ye
' ſhall ſay, Bleſſed is he that cometh in the name of
' the Lord;' the very cry at which the Scribes and
Phariſees were ſo much offended in the children,
when Jeſus entered Jeruſalem. This very cry would
then be that of the whole nation.

But though our Saviour could not fix the time of
his ſecond coming, or the commencement of his
proper kingdom, he ſufficiently forewarned his diſciples of the ſigns of its approach, and of ſome circumſtances that will immediately precede it, to which it
certainly behoves us to be attentive.

Before this great event the goſpel is to be preached

ed to all the world. Mat. xxiv. 14. ‘ And this gofpel
‘ of the kingdom fhall be preached through all the
‘ world, for a witnefs to all nations, and then fhall the
‘ end come.’ If by the whole world, we mean the
Roman empire, this was accomplifhed before the
deftruction of Jerufalem, and therefore may refer to
that event. But it may have a farther reference, and
now there is hardly any nation that has not had an
opportunity of having the gofpel preached to them;
and the late wonderful extenfion of navigation, by
which the whole of the habitable world has been ex-
plored by Chriftians, though this was by no means
the object of the navigators, will, no doubt, be the
means of carrying the knowledge of the gofpel to a
greater extent than ever; and the troubles of Europe
will greatly contribute to the fame end. Times of
trouble make men ferious. With thefe ferious im-
preffions on their minds many will fly to diftant
countries, and carry the knowledge of the gofpel
with them; and, it may be hoped, in greater purity,
and confequently more worthy of their acceptance,
than it has hitherto appeared to them.

Another preceding event, and of a more definite
kind, is the great prevalence of infidelity, Luke
xviii. 8. ‘ When the Son of Man cometh, fhall he
‘ find faith in the earth.’ Now the prevalence of infidelity of late years has been very remarkable in all
countries in which antichriftian hierarchies have been
eftablifhed. And certainly all civil eftablifhments of
Chriftianity, in which power is claimed to prefcribe

articles of faith, to make laws to bind the conſciences of Chriſtians, and inflict temporal puniſhments for the violation of them, are properly antichriſtian. For, as Chriſtians, we are commanded to acknowledge no man maſter upon earth, ſince one is our maſter, even Chriſt.

Moreover, ſuch abſurd doctrines have been eſtabliſhed by human authority, and ſuch horrid puniſhments have been inflicted upon men for obeying the dictates of conſcience, under all thoſe hierarchies, proteſtant ones not excepted, that the minds of men have revolted at them; and, ſhocked at ſuch enormities, have thrown off the belief and profeſſion of Chriſtianity altogether. This was long ago the caſe in Italy, where the enormities of the court of Rome were the moſt conſpicuous; and many of the cardinals, and ſome of the popes themſelves, are well known to have been unbelievers.

That this has long been the caſe in France, is what no perſon acquainted with that country the laſt fifty years will deny. It is now become more generally known, becauſe it has had a better opportunity of ſhewing itſelf. That, in ſimilar circumſtances, the ſame, or ſomething approaching to it, would not appear to be the caſe with *us*, is more than thoſe who are acquainted with the ſtate of things in this reſpect will vouch for.

When I was myſelf in France in 1774, I ſaw ſufficient reaſon to believe, that hardly any perſon of eminence, in church or ſtate, and eſpecially in the leaſt degree eminent in philoſophy, or literature,

(whoſe

(whofe opinions in all countries are, fooner or later, adopted by others) were believers in Chriftianity; and no perfon will fuppofe that there has been any change in favour of Chriftianity in the laft twenty years. A perfon, I believe now living, and one of the beft informed men in the country, affured me, very gravely, that (paying me a compliment) I was the firft perfon he had ever met with, of whofe un-derftanding he had any opinion, who pretended to believe Chriftianity. To this all the company affent-ed. And not only were the philofophers, and other leading men in France, at that time unbelievers in Chriftianity, or deifts, but *atheifts*, denying the being of a God. Nay Voltaire himfelf, who was then living, was confidered by them as a weak-minded man, be-caufe, though an unbeliever in revelation, he believed in a God.

When I afked thefe gentlemen what it was that appeared to them fo incredible in Chriftianity, that they rejected it without farther examination (for they did not pretend to have employed much time on the fubject) they mentioned the doctrines of tran-fubftantiation, and the trinity, as things too palpably abfurd to require any difcuffion. It is, without doubt, the civil eftablifhment of fuch Chriftianity as this, at which the common fenfe of mankind will ever revolt, that makes fo many unbelievers of perfons who will not take the trouble to read the fcriptures for them-felves, or who have not fagacity or patience to fee through the falfe gloffes that have been fo long put upon them. Theſe ſyſtems, and the blindneſs and obſtinacy in the governing-powers, in rejecting every propoſal of reforming the moſt palpable abuſes, and the moſt manifeſt oppreſſions, make unbelievers much faſter than all rational Chriſtians can unmake them.

Nothing, however, can ever counteract the fatal influence of ſuch corrupt Chriſtianity, as is ſupported by theſe hierarchies, which are 'alſo intolerably ex-penſive and oppreſſive, but the exhibition of rational Chriſtianity, with its proper evidence, by unitarian Chriſtians. But theſe are yet ſo few, compared with the bulk of Chriſtians, who are trinitarians, that ſuperficial obſervers, as unbelievers in general 'are, who judge by the great maſs, pay but little regard to their repreſentations.

Happily, this infidelity is, in its turn, deſtroying thoſe antichriſtian eſtabliſhments which gave birth to it; and when this great revolution ſhall be accom-pliſhed, genuine unadulterated chriſtianity, meeting with leſs obſtruction, will not fail to recommend and eſtabliſh itſelf by its own evidence, and become the religion of the whole world. True Chriſtianity ſtands in no need of the aid of civil power.

This was the idea of the great Sir Iſaac Newton, as appears from the evidence of the excellent Mr. Whiſton, in the following paſſage of his *Eſſay on the Revelation*, 2d edition, p. 321. " Sir Iſaac Newton " had a very ſagacious conjecture, which he told

" Dr.

" Dr. Clarke, from whom I received it, that the
" overbearing tyranny and perfecuting power of the
" antichriftian party, which hath fo long corrupted
" Chriftianity, and enflaved the Chriftian world,
" muft be put a ftop to, and broken to pieces by the
" prevalence of infidelity, for fome time, before pri-
" mitive Chriftianity could be reftored; which feems
" to be the very means that is now working in Eu-
" rope, for the fame good and great end of Pro-
" vidence. Poffibly he might think that our Sa-
" viour's own words implied it: When the Son of
" Man cometh fhall he find faith on the earth?
" Luke xviii. 8. See Conftitut. Apoft. vi. 18;
" vii. 32; or poffibly he might think no other way
" fo likely to do it in human affairs; it being, I
" acknowledge, too fadly evident, that there is not
" at prefent religion enough in Chriftendom, to put
" a ftop to fuch antichriftian tyranny and perfecution,
" upon any genuine principles of Chriftianity."

The concluding obfervation of Mr. Whifton appears to me to be very juft. It feems probable that
no Chriftians, not even the freeft, and boldeft, would
ever have done what was neceffary to be done, to
the overturning of thefe corrupt eftablifhments of
Chriftianity, that unbelievers have lately done in
France.

This great event of the late revolution in France
appears to me, and many others, to be not improba-
bly the accomplifhment of the following part of the
Revelation,

Revelation, chap. xi. 3. ' And the ſame hour there
' was a great earthquake, and the tenth part of the
' city fell, and in the earthquake were ſlain of men
' (or literally, *names of men)* ſeven thouſand, and the
' remnant were affrighted, and gave glory to God.'

An earthquake, as I have obſerved, may ſignify a
great convulſion, and revolution, in ſtates; and as the
Papal dominions were divided into ten parts, one of
which, and one of the principal of them, was France,
it is properly called *a tenth part of the city,* or of the
myſtical *Babylon.* And if by *names of men,* we un-
derſtand their *titles,* ſuch as thoſe of the nobility, and
other hereditary diſtinctions, all of which are now
aboliſhed, the accompliſhment of the prediction will
appear to be wonderfully exact. It is farther remarkable, that this paſſage immediately precedes what I have
quoted before concerning the *nations being angry,* and
the wrath of God being come, for the *deſtruction of
thoſe who have deſtroyed the earth.*

It is farther remarkable, that the kings of France
were thoſe who gave the Popes their temporalities,
and the rank they now hold among the princes of the
world. And it is foretold, Rev. xvii. 16, that ' thoſe
' kings who gave their power and ſtrength unto the
' beaſt, theſe ſhall hate the whore, and ſhall make
' her deſolate and naked, and ſhall eat her fleſh, and
' burn her with fire. For God has put it in their
' hearts to fulfil his will, and to agree to give their
' kingdoms unto the beaſt, until the words of God
' ſhall be fulfilled.'

May

May we not hence conclude it to be highly probable, that what has taken place in Franee will be
done in other countries? But the total deftruction
of this great antichriftian power feems to be referved
for the fecond coming of Chrift in perfon, by the
brightnefs of whofe appearance, and not before, he is,
according to the apoftle Paul, to be completely *deftroyed.* And with this view, as well as others, every
Proteftant Chriftian fhould fay, ' Come, Lord Jefus,
' come quickly.' In the mean time, let us attend to
the folemn admonition in the Revelation xviii. 4.
' I heard a voice from heaven, faying, Come out of
' her, my people, that ye be not partakers of her fins,
' and that ye receive not of her plagues. For her
' fins have reached unto heaven, and God hath re-
' membered her iniquities *.'

---

* That the opinion here advanced, concerning the danger of
the civil powers of Europe, in confequence of their connexion
with antichriftian ecclefiaftical fyftems, has been long enter-
tained by me, may appear from the following extract from my
Hiftory of the Corruptions of Chriftianity, vol. ii. p. 484. " It is no-
" thing but the alliance of the kingdom of Chrift with the king-
" doms of this world (an alliance which our Lord himfelf ex-
" prefsly difclaimed) that fupports the groffeft corruptions of
" Chriftianity; and perhaps we muft wait for the fall of the civil
" powers before this moft unnatural alliance be broken. Cala-
" mitous, no doubt, will that time be. But what convulfion in
" the political world ought to be a fubject of lamentation, if it
" be attended with fo defirable an event? May the kingdom of
" God, and of Chrift, (that which I conceive to be intended
" in the Lord's Prayer) truly and fully come, though all the
" kingdoms of the world be removed in order to make way for
" it."

As

As the ſecond coming of Chriſt will be during the general prevalence of infidelity, ſo it will be ſudden, and moſt unexpected. This is the language of our Saviour himſelf, Mat. xxiv. 37. 'As the days of ' Noah were, ſo ſhall the coming of the Son of Man ' be. For as in the days before the flood, they were ' eating, and drinking, marrying, and giving in mar- ' riage, unto the day that Noah entered into the ark, ' and knew not till the flood came, and took them ' all away, ſo ſhall alſo the coming of the Son of ' Man be.' Luke xvii. 28. 'Likewiſe, alſo as it ' was in the days of Lot. They did eat, they drank, ' they bought, they ſold, they planted, they builded. ' But the ſame day that Lot went out of Sodom, he ' rained fire and brimſtone from heaven, and de- ' ſtroyed them all. Even thus ſhall it be when the ' Son of Man is revealed.' The apoſtle Paul alſo ſays, 1 Theſ. v. 2. 'Yourſelves know perfectly, ' that the day of the Lord ſo cometh as a thief in ' the night. For when they ſhall ſay peace and ' ſafety, then ſudden deſtruction cometh upon them, ' as travail upon a woman with child, and they ſhall ' not eſcape.'

But ſudden and unexpected as the coming of Chriſt will be, it will be moſt conſpicuous. Speaking of his return, he ſays, Mat. xxiv. 26. 'If they ſhall ' ſay unto you, Behold he' (i. e. the Meſſiah) 'is in ' the deſert, go not forth. Behold he is in the ſecret ' chambers, believe it not. For as the lightning ' cometh out of the eaſt; and ſhineth even unto the ' weſt,

' weſt, ſo ſhall alſo the coming of the Son of Man
' be.' As the aſcent of Jeſus was conſpicuous, and
probably leiſurely, ſo will be his deſcent. While
the diſciples were viewing him as he aſcended, we
read, Acts i. 10, ' two men ſtood by them in white
' apparel, who alſo ſaid, Ye men of Galilee, why
' ſtand ye gazing up into heaven?. This ſame Jeſus,
' who is taken from you into heaven, ſhall ſo come in
' like manner as ye have ſeen him go into heaven.'
Here is no figurative language, no ambiguous ex-
preſſion. Neither is there in what the apoſtle ſays
concerning the reſurrection of the virtuous dead,
which will take place at the coming of Chriſt,
which, in the Revelation is called *the firſt reſurrec-*
tion, 1 Theſ. iv. 14. ' If we believe that Jeſus died,
' and roſe again, even ſo them alſo who ſleep in Je-
' ſus ſhall God bring with him. For this we ſay
' unto you, by the word of the Lord, that we who
' are alive, and remain unto the coming of the Lord,
' ſhall have no advantage over thoſe who are aſleep.
' For the Lord himſelf ſhall deſcend from heaven,
' with a ſhout, with the voice of the archangel, and
' with the trump of God, and the dead in Chriſt
' ſhall riſe firſt. Then we who are alive, and re-
' main, ſhall be caught up together with them in the
' clouds, to meet the Lord in the air, and ſo ſhall
' we ever be with the Lord.' Again he ſays, 1 Cor.
xv. 51. ' We ſhall not all ſleep, but we ſhall all be
' changed, in a moment, in the twinkling of an eye,
' at the laſt trump. For the trumpet ſhall ſound, and
                                                    ' the

' the dead ſhall be raiſed incorruptible, and we ſhall
' be changed.'

The certainty of this great cataſtrophe ſhould be
a ſufficient motive with all Chriſtians, who, as ſuch,
entertain no doubt with reſpect to the fact, to keep it
conſtantly in view, and to regulate their whole conduct with a view to it. But if we apprehend it to be
in a ſtricter ſenſe of the word really *near*, which, from
the preſent aſpect of things, I own I am inclined to
think may be the caſe, our attention is drawn to it in
a moſt forcible manner. Did we really expect to ſee
this great event, viz. the coming of Chriſt in the
clouds of heaven, we ſhould hardly think or ſpeak of
any thing elſe; and the preſent commotions in the
political world, extraordinary as they certainly are,
would appear as nothing in compariſon with it:
What would otherwiſe be *great*, would, with reſpect
to this, ſeem exceedingly *little*, and inſignificant.

What then, my brethren, is the practical inference
that we ſhould draw from finding, or even ſuſpect-
ing, ourſelves to be in this ſituation, the kingdom of
heaven being at hand, but to repent, and by a
change of heart and of life to be prepared for it; that
' when our Lord ſhall return, and take an account
' of his ſervants, we may be found of him without
' ſpot and blamelefs, and not be aſhamed before him
' at his coming?' 'Seeing,' as the apoſtle Peter ſays,
' we look for theſe things, what manner of perſons
' ought we to be, in all holy converſation and god-
' lineſs.'

The

'The afpect of things, it cannot be denied, is, in the higheft degree, alarming, making life, and every thing in it, peculiarly uncertain. · What could have been more unexpected than the events of any one of the laft four years, at the beginning of it? What a total revolution in the ideas, and conduct of a whole nation! What a total fubverfion of principles, what reverfes of fortune, and what a wafte of life! In how bloody and eventful a war are we engaged, how inconfiderable in its beginning, how rapid and wide in its progrefs, and how dark with refpect to its termination! At firft it refembled Elijah's cloud, appearing no bigger than a *man's hand*; but now it covers, and darkens, the whole European hemifphere!

Now, whatever we may think, as politicians (and with us every man will have his own opinion, on a fubject fo interefting to us all) I would, in this place, admonifh you not to overlook the hand of God in √ the great fcene that is now opening upon us. Nothing can ever come to pafs without his appointment, or permiffion; and then, whatever be the views of men, we cannot doubt, but that his are always wife, righteous, and good. Let us, therefore, exercife faith in him, believing that though 'clouds and darknefs are ' round about him, righteoufnefs and judgment are ' for ever the habitation of his throne.' All thofe who appear on the theatre of public affairs, in the field, or the cabinet, both thofe whom we praife, and thofe whom we blame, are equally inftruments in his hands, and execute all his pleafure. Let this reflection,

tion, then, in our cooler moments, (and I hope we
ſhall endeavour, in all the tumult of affairs, to make
theſe as many as poſſible) lead us to look more to
God, and leſs to man; and conſequently, in all the
troubles in which we may be involved, repoſe the
moſt unſhaken confidence in him, and thence 'in
' patience poſſeſs our own ſouls,' eſpecially when it is
evident that it is wholly out of our power to alter
the courſe of events. If we be careful ſo to live as
to be at all times prepared to die, what have we to
fear, even though, as the Pſalmiſt ſays, the ' earth be
' removed, and the mountains be carried into the
' midſt of the ſea?' Whatever turn the courſe of
things may take, it cannot then be to our diſadvan-
tage. What, then, ſhould hinder our contemplating
the great ſcene, that ſeems now to be opening upon
us, awful as it is, with tranquillity, and even with ſa-
tisfaction, from our firm perſuaſion, that its termination will be glorious and happy?

Laſtly, the more there are who indulge theſe enlarged and juſt views, who cultivate a ſenſe of piety
to God (which will always lead us to ſuppreſs reſentment, and to promote goodwill towards men) the
more favour, in the righteous adminiſtration of Providence, will be ſhewn to the country in which they
ſhall be found God, we know, would have ſpared
even Sodom, if ſo many as ten righteous men had
been found in it; and our Saviour, alluding, as I am
inclined to think, to theſe very times, which ſeem to
be approaching, ſays, that ' for the elect's ſake they

' will

' will be fhortened.' For our own fakes, therefore, for the fake of our friends, of our country, and of every thing that is dear to us in it, let us attend to the admonition of my text, ' to repent, for the ' kingdom of heaven is at hand.' It is ' righteouf- ' nefs that exalteth a nation', and ' fin' only is the ' reproach,' and will be the ruin, ' of any people.'

APPENDIX.

H a v i n g originally got the leading ideas that are enlarged upon in the preceding difcourfe from *Dr. Hartley's Obfervations on Man,* a work publifhed in 1749, I think it may not be amifs to fubjoin to it fome extracts from that work, as, from his authority, the ferious apprehenfions with which I have, ever fince I read it, been impreffed, will receive more weight, than they could acquire from any perfon, who, writing in thefe times, might be fuppofed to be particularly influenced by the afpect of them, and by his own fituation with refpect to them. I wifh like-wife by this, as well as every other means, to direct the attention of my readers to that moft excellent work, to which I am indebted, if I may fo fay, for the whole moral conformation of my mind.

" How near the diffolution of the prefent governments, generally or particularly, may be, would be great rafhnefs to affirm. Chrift will come in this fenfe alfo ' as a thief in the night.' Our duty is there-fore to watch and to pray; to be faithful ftewards; to give meat, and all other requifites, in due feafon, to thofe under our care; and to endeavour by thefe, and all other lawful means, to preferve the government, under whofe protection we live, from dif-

folution,

.folution, feeking the peace of it, and fubmitting to every ordinance of man for the Lord's fake. No prayers, no endeavours of this kind can fail of having fome good effect, public or private, for the prefervation of ourfelves and others. The great difpenfations of Providence are conducted by means that are either fecret, or, if they appear, that are judged feeble and inefficacious.—No man can tell, however private his ftation may be, but his fervent prayer may avail to the falvation of much people. But it is more peculiarly the duty of magiftrates thus to watch over their fubjects, to pray for them, and to fet about the reformation of all matters civil and ecclefiaftical, to the utmoft of their power. Good governors may promote the welfare and continuance of a ftate, and wicked ones muft accelerate its ruin."

" The facred hiftory affords us inftances of both kinds, and they are recorded there for the admonition of kings and princes in all future times." V. ii. p. 368.

" There are many prophecies which declare the fall of the ecclefiaftical powers of the Chriftian world. And though each church feems to flatter itfelf with the hopes of being exempted; yet it is very plain that the prophetical characters belong to all. They have all left the true, pure, fimple religion, and teach for doctrines the commandments of men. They are all merchants of the earth, and have fet up a kingdom of this world, abounding in riches, temporal power, and external pomp. They have all a dogmatizing fpirit, and perfecute fuch as do not

receive

receive their own mark, and worſhip the image
which they have ſet up. They all neglect Chriſt's
command of preaching the goſpel to all nations, and
even that of going to ' the loſt ſheep of the houſe of
' Iſrael;' there being innumerable multitudes in all
Chriſtian countries who have never been taught to
read, and who are in other reſpects alſo deſtitute of
the means of ſaving knowledge. 'Tis very true that
the church of Rome is ' Babylon the great and the
' mother of harlots,' and of the ' abominations of the
' earth.' But all the reſt have copied her example
more or leſs. They have all received money like
Gehazi; and therefore the leproſy of *Naaman* will
cleave to them, and to their ſeed for ever. And this
impurity may be conſidered, not only as juſtifying the
application of the prophecies to all the Chriſtian
churches, but as a natural cauſe for their downfall.
The corrupt governors of the ſeveral churches will
ever oppoſe the true goſpel, and in ſo doing will
bring ruin upon themſelves." P. 371.

" As the downfall of the Jewiſh ſtate under Titus
was the occaſion of the publication of the goſpel to
us Gentiles, ſo our downfall may contribute to the
reſtoration of the Jews, and both together bring on
the final publication and prevalence of the true religion. Thus the type and the thing typified will
coincide. The firſt fruits and the lump are made
holy together." P. 375.

" The downfall of the civil and ecclefiaſtical
powers muſt both be attended with ſuch public
calamities, as will make men ſerious, and alſo

D 3   drive

drive them from the countries of *Chriftendom* into the remote parts of the world, particularly into the Eaft and Weft-Indies; whither, confequently, they will carry their religion, now purified from errors and fuperftitions." P. 77.

" That worldly-mindednefs, and neglect of duty in the clergy, muft haften our ruin, cannot be doubt-ed. Thefe are ' the falt of the earth,' and the ' light ' of the world.' If they lofe their favour, the whole nation, where this happens, will be converted into one putrid mafs. If their light become darknefs, the whole body politic muft be dark alfo. The de-generacy of the court of *Rome*, and fecular bifhops abroad, are too notorious to be mentioned. They almoft ceafe to give offence, as they fcarce pretend to any function or authority befides what is temporal. Yet ftill there is great mockery of God in their ex-ternal pomp, and profanation of facred titles; which, fooner or later, will bring down vengeance upon them. And as the court of Rome has been at the head of the great apoftafy, and corruption of the Chriftian church; and feems evidently marked out in various places of the fcriptures, the fevereft judg-ments are probably referved for her. But I rather choofe to fpeak to what falls under the obfervation of all ferious, attentive perfons in this kingdom. The fuperior clergy are in general, ambitious, and eager in the purfuit of riches; flatterers of the great, and fubfervient to party intereft; negligent of their own immediate charges, and alfo of the inferior clergy,

and,

and their immediate charges.. The inferior clergy. imitate their fuperiors, and in general take little more care of their parifhes than barely what is ne-ceffary to avoid the cenfure of the law. And the. clergy of all ranks are, in general, either ignorant, or if they do apply, it is rather to profane learning, to philofophical or political matters, than to the: ftudy of the fcriptures, of the Oriental languages, of. the fathers, and ecclefiaftical authors, and of the writings of devout men in different ages of the church. I fay this is in general the cafe; i. e. far the greater part of the clergy of all ranks in this kingdom are of this kind. But there are fome of a quite different character; men eminent for piety, facred learning, and the faithful difcharge of their duty, and who, it is not to be doubted, mourn in fecret for the crying fins of this and other nations. The clergy, in general, are alfo far more free from open and grofs vices, than any other denomination of men amongft us, phyficians, lawyers, merchants, foldiers, &c. However, this may be otherwife hereafter. For it is faid. that in fome foreign coun-tries the fuperior clergy, in others the inferior, are as corrupt and abandoned, or more fo, than any other order of men. The clergy in this kingdom feem to be what one might expect from the mixture of. good and bad influences that affect them. But then, if we make this candid allowance for *them*, we muft alfo make it for perfons in the high ranks of life, for their infidelity, lewdnefs, and fordid felf-intereft.

I   And

And though it becomes an humble, charitable and impartial man, to make all thefe allowances, yet he cannot but fee, that the judgments of God are ready to fall upon us all for thefe things; and that they may fall firft, and with the greateft weight, upon thofe, who, having the higheft office committed to them in the fpiritual kingdom of Chrift, neglect it, and are become mere ' merchants of the ' earth,' and ' fhepherds that feed themfelves, and ' not their flocks.' P. 450.

" Thefe are my real and earneft fentiments upon thefe points. It would be great rafhnefs to fix a time for the breaking of the ftorm that hangs over our heads, as it is blindnefs and infatuation not to fee it; nor to be aware, that it may break. And yet this infatuation has always attended all falling ftates. The kingdoms of Judah and Ifrael, which are the types of all the reft, were thus infatuated. It may be, that the prophecies concerning Edom, Moab, Ammon, Tyre, Egypt, &c. will become applicable to particular kingdoms before their fall, and warn the good to flee out of them. And Chriftendom in general feems ready to affume to itfelf the place and lot of the Jews, after they had rejected their Meffiah, the Saviour of the world. Let no one deceive himfelf, or others. The prefent circumftances of the world are extraordinary and critical, beyond what has ever yet happened. If we refufe to let Chrift reign over us, as our Redeemer and Saviour, we muft be flain before his face, as enemies, at his fecond coming." 455.

To

To thefe paffages from Dr. Hartley, I fhall add another from an excellent *Sermon preached in the chapel of Trinity College, Cambridge, December* 13, 1793, *the day appointed for the commemoration of the Benefactors to that Society.* p. 13, &c.

" Nature recoils with horror at the fpectacle now prefented by their unfortunate country [France]. Under the guidance, however, of divine revelation, the contemplative mind may difcern the figns of thefe times, and the hand of Providence directing the madnefs of the people. The oracles of truth, when foretelling the perfecutions to be endured by Chriftians, affure us, ' He that killeth with the ' fword, muft be killed with the fword.' *They have fhed* (faith the angel) *the blood of faints and prophets, and thou haft given them blood to drink; for they are worthy.* Deftruction awaits the perfecutor. And it muft excite our aftonifhment to fee veftiges of this righteous difpenfation in what is paffing before us. Lyons is recorded in early hiftory, as the fpot where a company of Martyrs glorified God. Lyons is now devoted, and its name erafed from the memory of man. Paris once ftreamed with the blood of the Hugonots: Paris hath fince been dyed with the flaughter of that court and clergy, which inftigated the unutterable deed."

" Let us, too, be honeft in declaring, whether if the maffacre of Saint Bartholomew, the revocation of the edict of Nantz, or a Spanifh act of faith, were dictated by the fpirit of Antichrift; the deprivation

of

of the TWO THOUSAND ejected Minifters; the fe-
verities which forced our countrymen to take re-
fuge in the wilds of America, and the two religious
conflagrations which have difgraced our own days,
demonftrated the prefiding influence of a mind like
that which was in Jefus."

" One particular in which the prophecy appears
to enlighten us, is the fate of the Gallican church.
The revolted city of the apocalypfe is fuppofed to
reprefent the Antichriftian community eftablifhed in
the European territory of the weftern Roman empire, ftill fubfifting in its pollarchical and difmem-
bered ftate. Of this city it is written, that the fall
of a tenth part would a fhort time precede that of
the reft; and that its overthrow would be accompa-
nied by an earthquake, and the deftruction of *feven
chiliads of the names of men.* As France was one of
the ten kingdoms founded on the ruins of the weftern empire; as violent commotions are now agitat-
ing the political world, from the Boryfthenes to the
Atlantic; as feven claffes have lately been deprived
of their privileges and titles; the curiofity of the
Chriftian fcholar is beyond meafure excited; and
will be gratified with the difcovery of various circumftances which will confirm his faith; but which
a defire of brevity obliges me to refer to his private
confideration. One queftion, however, I cannot help
propofing; that if *we* be of that chofen people who
have in truth come out of Babylon, who partake not
of her fins, and merit not her plagues, why fhould we
                                                    appear

appear unprepared, or difinclined, to comply with the angelic mandate, and begin, at leaft, fome prelude to that fong of triumph, ‘ Rejoice over her, ‘ thou heaven, and ye holy apoftles, and prophets, ‘ for God hath avenged you on her.’

" The legiflators of France are Deifts! While " they expatiated freely in every region of ufeful " fcience, they were enjoined to " *take for granted*" " thofe controverfial matters of religion, their fore- " fathers had fome good reafon for adhering to *." —" They were not permitted to diftinguifh the doctrines of our Lord from thofe of their church. Their mind arrived at maturity in fome points, difdained the puerilities on which they dared not fpeculate; and rejected the gofpel, on account of the meretricious drefs in which it was introduced to them."

" The legiflators of France are deifts! Much as we may lament their infidelity in their private capacity, we rejoice that, as lawgivers, they are unbelievers. Indifferent alike to all profeffions, and all fects, they will not form an unnatural alliance with one, nor profcribe all others with civil incapacities, imprifonment, and death. Every perfuafion will enjoy their equal and wife protection; and genuine Chriftianity, undifguifed with abfurd confeffions, and not made contemptible by ridiculous ceremonies, will exert her

* This is quoted from a fpeech of Dr. Milner, Vice-Chancellor of the Univerfity of Cambridge, on the trial of Mr. Fread.

proper

proper energies; will prefent to the underftanding of the individual her miraculous credentials of prophecies completed in our time; and gain her eftablifhment, not in word, but in deed; not in the civil code, but in the heart; not as a neceffary engine of the ftate, but as the truth, and the way to eternal life. Superftition will no longer "rear her mitred front in "their courts and parliaments *;" but the dominion of Chrift, triumphant in that country, will be an earneft of his obtaining the ' heathen for his inheritance, ' and the uttermoft parts of the earth for his pof- ' feffion.'

* Alluding to Mr. Burke's encomium on the Church of England.

THE END.